WITHDRAWN

BLAZERS

DIRT BIKE WORLD

Motocross Racing

by Thomas K. Adamson

Reading Consultant:
Barbara J. Fox
Reading Specialist
North Carolina State University

CAPSTONE PRESS
a capstone imprint

Blazers is published by Capstone Press,
151 Good Counsel Drive, P.O. Box 669, Mankato, Minnesota 56002.
www.capstonepub.com

Printed in the United States of America in North Mankato, Minnesota.
032010
005740CGF10

 Books published by Capstone Press are manufactured with paper
containing at least 10 percent post-consumer waste.

Library of Congress Cataloging-in-Publication Data
Adamson, Thomas K., 1970–
  Motocross racing/ by Thomas K. Adamson.
    p. cm.—(Blazers. dirt bike world.)
  Includes bibliographical references and index.
  Summary: "Describes motocross, including rules, course details, and stars
of the sport"—Provided by publisher.
  ISBN 978-1-4296-5018-2 (library binding)
  ISBN 978-1-4296-5629-0 (paperback)
  1. Motocross—Juvenile literature. I. Title. II. Series.

  GV1060.12.A38 2011
  796.7'56—dc22   2010004166

Editorial Credits
Mandy Robbins, editor; Tracy Davies, designer; Laura Manthe, production specialist

**Capstone Press would like to thank Ken Glaser, Director of Special Projects for the Motorcycle
Safety Foundation in Irvine, California, for his expertise and assistance in making this book.**

Photo Credits
Alamy/James Clews, 18, 19
AP Images/HO/Larry Lawrence, 17
CORBIS/Jonathan Selkowitz, 8; NewSport/Ben Burgeson, 15; NewSport/Steve Boyle, 22
Getty Images Inc/Christian Pondella, 21, 25; Steve Bruhn, 26, 27
Newscom, 5, 6, 7, 13, 16, 23, 24, 28–29; Imago, 10
Shutterstock/CTR Photos, cover, back cover

Artistic Effects
Shutterstock/Irmak Akcadogan, Konstanttin, Nitipong Ballapavanich, oriontrail

Table of Contents

chapter 1

Chase for the Title

The American Motorcyclist Association (AMA) Pro Motocross Championship was on the line. On August 22, 2009, Chad Reed saw his chance to win it.

Fact: Riders try to get the **holeshot**. This position gives them a better chance to win.

holeshot—the position held by the first rider through the first turn of a race

Davi Millsaps had a huge lead in the first **moto**. Reed slowly caught up, but he couldn't pass. Millsaps won the first moto. But Reed came back. He won the second moto and took the title.

Chad Reed

moto—one of tw
a motocross event

chapter 2

The Track and Gear

All motocross (MX) tracks are different. But each track tests riders. Large jumps send riders sailing through the air. Smaller **whoops** challenge them to control their bikes.

whoops—low bumps that are close together on the track

Crashes are a common sight in MX. Riders stay safe by wearing sturdy boots and helmets. They also wear body **armor**. Goggles protect riders from getting dirt in their eyes.

armor—hard covering riders wear for protection in crashes

Dirt bikes are built to handle rough courses. Knobby tires grip the dirt. Bikes also have strong **suspension** systems. They help riders land safely after jumps.

Fact: Women get in on the racing action too. Jessica Patterson has won five national championships in women's MX.

suspension—a system of springs and shock absorbers that softens a dirt bike's up-and-down movements

chapter 3

Pro Racing

The AMA Pro Motocross Championship is the top MX series in the United States. This series hosts 12 events each year.

Fact: AMA pro races have two classes—250cc and 450cc. Classes are based on engine size. The "cc" stands for cubic centimeters.

Each event has two motos. Riders earn points based on how they finish. The rider with the most points wins.

Ricky Carmichael celebrating a victory

Fact: In AMA pro races, each moto lasts 30 minutes plus two additional laps.

The Motocross of Nations was first held in 1947. It is the biggest off-road motorcycle race in the world. At least 30 countries send their three best racers to this event.

Team USA celebrating victory at the 2008 Motocross of Nations

Fact: U.S. teams have won the Motocross of Nations more times than any other team.

chapter 4

MX Stars

Jeremy McGrath raced in **supercross** (SX) and MX during the 1990s. He had 15 wins in the MX 250cc class. McGrath's exciting racing style brought more fans to the sport.

supercross—motorcycle races held on dirt tracks in stadiums

Jeremy McGrath

Before he retired in 2007, Ricky Carmichael was the rider to beat. He had perfect seasons in both the 250cc and 450cc classes. Carmichael won the SX and MX championships in the same season five times.

Ricky Carmichael

Chad Reed was an SX champion in Australia. In 2002, he moved to the United States to race in SX and MX. In 2009, he won the MX 450cc class championship.

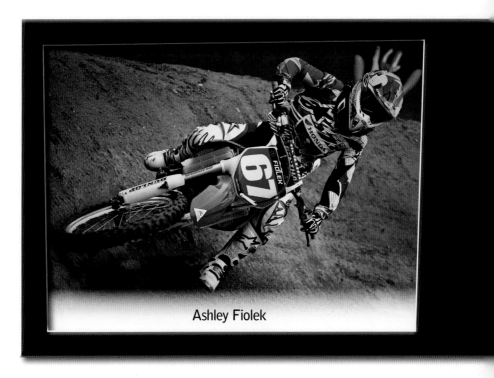

Ashley Fiolek

Fact: Ashley Fiolek was the 2009 AMA Women's Motocross champion. She won the title while racing with a broken collarbone.

James Stewart began racing in the 450cc MX class in 2006. In 2008, he had a perfect season, matching Carmichael's achievement. Stars like Stewart, Reed, and Carmichael keep fans hooked on MX.

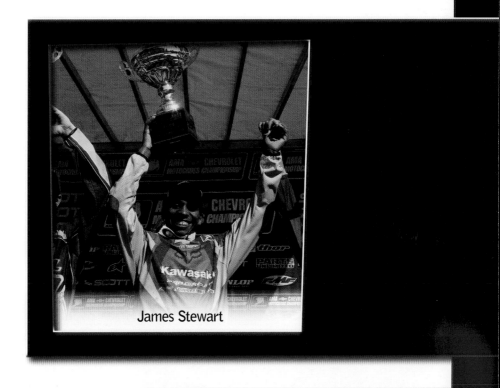

James Stewart

Fact: In 2002, Stewart won the AMA Rookie of the Year award. He was only 16.

Moto Mud!

Glossary

armor (AR-muhr)—hard covering riders wear for protection in crashes

holeshot (HOLE-shot)—the position held by the first rider through the first turn of a race

moto (MOH-toh)—a single motocross race; each motocross event includes two motos

supercross (SOO-puhr-kross)—motorcycle races held on dirt tracks in stadiums

suspension (suh-SPEN-shuhn)—a system of springs and shock absorbers that absorbs a dirt bike's up-and-down movements

whoops (WOOPS)—low bumps that are close together on an MX or SX track

Read More

Armentrout, David, and Patricia Armentrout. *On the Tracks.* Motorcycle Mania II. Vero Beach, Fla.: Rourke Publishing, 2008.

Perritano, John. *American MX: From Backwater to World Leaders.* New York: Crabtree Publishing Company, 2008.

Stealey, Bryan. *Motocross.* Racing Mania. New York: Marshall Cavendish Benchmark, 2010.

Internet Sites

FactHound offers a safe, fun way to find Internet sites related to this book. All of the sites on FactHound have been researched by our staff.

Here's all you do:

Visit *www.facthound.com*

FactHound will fetch the best sites for you!

Index